MW00916234

Top 10 FSBO Objections

FOR SALE BY OWNERS ARE THE FASTEST SOURCE OF BUSINESS OPPORTUNITY!

William J. May

Copyright © 2018 WillieJMayEnterprises.com

All rights reserved. No part of this book may be reproduced in any form, or by any electronic or mechanical means, including but not limited to information storage and retrieval systems, without written permission from the author. Only possible exception is by a reviewer, who may include short excerpts in a published review.

Willie J. May Enterprises edition 2018

Disclaimer: William J. May is a licensed real estate agent in Torrance, California. Printed in the USA. The information presented herein represents the views of the author as of the date of publication. This book is presented for informational purposes only. This book contains statistical examples.
It is understood, if you use these statistics, you need to know your own market. Real Estate is local, and every market is different. Due to the rate of which conditions change, the author reserves the right to alter and/or update this information based on new conditions. While every attempt has been made to verify the information in this book, neither the author nor his affiliates/partners assume any responsibility for errors, inaccuracies, or omissions. It is understood that the income statements and examples are not intended to represent or guarantee that anyone will achieve the same results. Each individual's success will be determined by his or her desire, dedication, background, skills, knowledge, effort, and motivation to work and follow recommendations. There is no guarantee you will duplicate the results stated. You recognize any business endeavor has an inherent risk for loss of capital.

More from This Author

Get William's #1 Amazon Best Selling Book Top 10 Expired Objections so you know what words to say and when to say them!
What Others Are Saying:
- "Easy read with a lot of useful information."
- "Awesome book on handling objections for expireds!"
- "Fantastic Playbook for Expireds"

Foreword

Man, I wish I had this book when I first started in real estate! I could have helped more people. I would have taken more listings… And made more money! Why? Because knowing WHAT to say to motivated prospects is half the battle. Yes, there are plenty of 'free' scripts and dialogs out there. But that's exactly the problem - using them will make you sound just like everybody else.

You already know that LISTINGS are the secret to success in this business.
Easiest and often fastest listings are expireds and FSBOs.

When it comes to objections, most of the stuff taught these days by all those gurus and trainers is essentially arguing with the prospect. It's uncomfortable and ineffective. If anything, it's a safe road to piss good prospects off and lose a chance to help them.

This book is different because it's written by my student and friend William May. William is an active agent who -- just like you is in the trenches every day: working, prospecting, following up, hustling.

I've known William for over six or seven years. He's a graduate from one of the most intense real estate training programs in the world: The "Double Your Listings Bootcamp".
William is a rockstar real estate agent in a ultra-competive market of Southern California.

The French say: "Never trust a skinny chef!" You want to learn the art of objection handling, then might as well learn it from someone who walks the walk just like you.

Getting this book was a smart choice. But it will only work if you implement it.

This is not a book to read. This is a workbook. A battle plan with answers to even the toughest FSBO objections.

Most agents don't work with FSBOs. Why? Mainly because they don't know what to say.
You're about to gain a huge advantage. This book will help you. Read it. Learn it. Practice it. Implement. Do it.

The best way to learn to ride a bike or any new skill for that matter, is to stop over thinking it, get your butt up on the seat and just start pedaling. At first it might feel a bit awkward and you might even fall down a couple times before you get the hang of it, but before you know it you'll be riding like a pro.

Same thing here. Your confidence will come from experience. Practice this stuff daily and watch how quickly positive results - leads and listings - can follow.

FSBOs can be your 'bread-and-butter' listings. Just look around. Majority of them end up listing with a competent agent. And knowing what to say, how to answer sellers' questions and handle their objections can make you that agent - a FSBO Rockstar.

Best of luck on your journey!

Borino
Your Real Estate Coach

Borino is the author of the 'no resistance' FSBO System for real estate agents "The FSBORINO": https://FSBORINO.com

Founder of one of the largest real estate groups for rockstar agents on Facebook: https://www.facebook.com/groups/rockstar.agents/

Introduction

You're driving down the street. You have your music playing in the background; it's a beautiful day with the sun shining and birds chirping, and suddenly off in the distance you see a little sign. As it comes into focus you realize it is a FOR SALE BY OWNER sign. You become a little nervous. You start shaking, and a lump form in your throat. You grip the steering wheel tighter as you slam on the gas to get away as quickly as you can.

In the back of your mind you know you should stop, pull over and go knock on that door! Yet you've been pre-programmed by other agents that FSBO sellers don't and won't respect you. They want to save the commission. Why should they hire you, when they could just sell their home themselves? And the excuses go on and on.

I'll be the first one to tell you that working with FSBO sellers is not for everyone, but every seller's situation is different. Let me ask you a quick question... How many people do you have to call, or doors do you have to knock on, to hit that ONE client who's looking to sell RIGHT NOW? Fifty, a hundred, maybe even a thousand?

We, as real estate agents, already know that it's a numbers game. I know this all too well, and that's why I love FSBO sellers! They're looking to sell NOW. So, what if they want to try it on their own? You can't blame them for trying. If there were a way for you to save tens of thousands of dollars on any kind of sale, you would most likely do it yourself as well, wouldn't you? Of course, you would.

We are in the DIY generation. We all want to try and do everything ourselves, and if we find out we can't, then we'll just hire a professional to clean up our mess. Those are the for sale by owner sellers that I look for. That regular Joe who tried to sell his home on his own but couldn't. Now he's ready for a professional to step in and get the job done, and that's where we come in.

This book is going to teach you that working with for sale by owner sellers is a courtship. It's not a slam, bam, thank you ma'am kind of business. I'll teach you the FSBO mindset, and the best follow-up system. I'll teach you how to develop a relationship, over time, that will help to establish a trust with your clients. I will also share with you my Top 10 For-Sale-By-Owner Objection Handlers, so that you'll know how to communicate with the FSBO seller, answer their questions, and overcome their objections in a nice caring manner, that puts both sellers and agents at ease.

Nothing in this life is guaranteed, so I'll just promise you this… After reading this book, you will no longer think of FSBO's as scary, terrifying home sellers. You will learn, understand, and realize that from now on in your financial future, the abbreviation of F.S.B.O will stand for "The Fastest Source of Business Opportunity!"

So, let's get started, ok?

Chapter 1: What Are Your Goals in Real Estate?

Before we get into the nitty-gritty details of working with FSBO sellers; knowing how to talk to them, reasoning with them, and overcoming their fears and objections, you must first have an understanding of what you are looking to get out of a career in real estate. What are YOUR goals and dreams?

Just so we're on the same page, I'm going keep it real. The real estate business is one of the hardest businesses known to man. It's a selling game, and most people just do not know how to sell. You're not really selling real estate, you're selling yourself. You're demonstrating to your potential client that you can get their house sold fast, for top dollar, and with the least amount of hassle. That's what it all boils down to -- your confidence and your willingness to go the extra mile to take care of business.

No matter what type of goals you have in real estate, in order to be successful and support your family you must follow a successful plan of action. For example: have an exit strategy. You should work towards purchasing income property for yourself once every year or two, so that when you retire from the real estate game, you'll have a passive income for years to come.

Another proactive way to be successful in real estate is to have a proven business model. Make a prospecting schedule, where you beat the pavement or make those cold calls. Have a lunch schedule that you stick to, so you may avoid too much downtime. Take time to study your real estate profession and learn your scripts and dialogs. That's digging in and getting to know your craft! Your hard work will pay off in the end.

You become what you focus on most of the time, so if you're focusing on being successful and learning your craft, eventually it will materialize.

Real estate is not a side gig. It is a full-time commitment. In the beginning you might need to do it part time as a means of supplemental income, and that's understandable. We all have to start somewhere. But every chance you get you need to be studying, learning, and getting to know your chosen profession. Hard work, determination and consistency are the fundamental keys to success. When you focus on the basics and you schedule your prospecting, it will become apparent that this is exactly how to make your dreams and goals come true.

SOLID GOLD TIP:
Prospect more than you think you should! Prospecting is the lifeblood of any successful real estate agent. If you do this, it will definitely change your life for the better. Trust me.

Chapter 2: F.E.A.R.

F.E.A.R. There are many acronyms for the word fear. For example: False Evidence Appears Real; Forgetting Everything About Reality; Future Events Already Ruined. Is that little word "fear" holding you back from greatness? Let me tell you, each and every real estate agent that you know, and even the mega agents that you don't know, have had to face fear at some point in their career.

Fear is definitely something I'm familiar with. When I was in school, the teacher would call upon me to answer a question. It didn't matter if I knew the answer or not, I was simply scared to death. I just had anxiety during certain situations. And don't even mention public speaking! Getting up in front of people and have them stare at you, waiting to see what you're going to say. For most people, public speaking is their number one fear. It can be more frightening than spiders, snakes, dogs or germs. Public speaking will put most people into a panic. But when it comes down to it, fear is really a good thing.

Fear protects us and warns us that danger is lurking. When I was in elementary school, I was terrified of going to my new classroom on the second floor. It was in an older building, and the stairs were on the outside of the building. I was very young at the time, and I was deathly afraid of heights! There was literally nothing the teachers could say or do to get me up those stairs and into that room. They called my mother and let her know that they would reassign me to a class on the first floor. When my father got home, he was having no part of it. You have to understand, my father was a Marine, and he believed that you can be afraid, hell, you can even be terrified, but to be a true warrior you had to overcome those emotions. Push through the fear.

He gave me a time frame. The first month it was understood that I would go to the reassigned first floor classroom, but every day I was to work on going up those stairs until I was able to get to the 2nd floor classroom. All that my father asked of me was to conquer two stairs a day. Two steps, that's it. As a son looking to please his father, I accepted. My father would question me every evening when he got home from work. Had I honored our agreement? Did I make my steps? He kept me on track, and within a week and a half I was in my new classroom. For the first month or two I was still fearful climbing those steps every day, but after a few months my fear had all but disappeared.

The best way to get over your fears is to confront them head-on. If you're scared about cold calling, meeting people, working with FSBO sellers, or anything else, the best way to overcome your fears is by facing them every day. Here are a few tips to make prospecting FSBO's, or just prospecting in general, easier.

Tips to Prospecting with Less Stress and Fear

Know Your Scripts and Objection Handlers

There's a reason why you run across real estate coaches who have been successful in teaching top producing agents how to be the best in their profession. It's because they stress upon their students the importance of learning their scripts and objection handlers. Because knowing what to say, and how to say it, will eventually transform you into a better real estate agent communicator.

Knowing how to interact with whatever prospect you're dealing with will be a huge boost to your confidence. You will have less fear, because you will know that whatever objection they throw at you, you can handle it. And you'll know in the worst-case scenario, if you do not close your prospect, that doesn't make you a bad agent. You're here to help them, and if they're not in the position to receive your help, you have a clear understanding of their needs. That maybe this is not the right time for them, or this is not a client you wish to work with. Or if the chemistry isn't right, maybe it's just best to move on to the next prospect.

When you use scripts to talk to potential clients, it keeps the conversation flowing and on track. In this way you can determine if the prospect is a potential client, or if they're just not interested right now. In other words, you're qualifying the prospect to see if they're in a position to sell and willing to work with you. Not to mention when you're using a good script you can double down and get to know the person and the situation that they're in more closely.

For example: What was their reason for moving into this particular neighborhood? What is the reason they're selling now? What do they like most about the neighborhood? How soon do they need to sell? How long will they try to sell on their own before they entertain other options?

Knowing, understanding, and implementing a good real estate script will excel your confidence, ignite your business, and put you ahead of your real estate competition. Real estate can be an easy business if you do not try to reinvent the wheel. Don't over-complicate things. Just follow the proven systems other successful real estate agents have used. All of them have some sort of script and objection handler they have used to be successful. They've done the research for you. You can simply use their tips and tricks to further your own success.

Know Your Business, Know Your Market Stats

One of the best ways to overcome fear and doubt, and boost your confidence in your real estate business, is to take your real estate business seriously. What do I mean by this? I mean by learning and knowing your trade. By following a set schedule every day to ensure success. By learning the contracts inside and out so you can best represent your client. Understand and know your local market stats in areas where you're prospecting. Know the average prices of homes sold in that area. Know the average days on market, average acreage, and the average square footage and number of bathrooms. Knowing this information without hesitation when speaking to a client will definitely make you an authority in the prospect's mind.

If you're new in the business or in a sales slump, look into adopting a mentor to help you with your real estate business. Look for a top producing agent in your office or area that has integrity and a character that you highly respect. Invite that agent out for coffee or lunch. You'll be surprised how most successful agents are willing to share their secrets to success and their systems with you. In my experience, low producing agents are the ones that are more secretive about their success.

Your mentor does not have to be an agent in your office. Your mentor could be anyone, anywhere across the country, but I would suggest trying to get a mentor that's easily accessible, willing to work with you, and who knows your local market. Listen to that agent, and shadow that agent if possible.

Understand that an agent's time is valuable. They're taking time out of their busy schedule to invest in your future, so whatever advice they give you, pay attention! Take notes and understand that it's going to take some time to learn it, to tweak it, to adapt it to fit your needs, and to adopt it for your business. Be patient! Rome was not built in one day.

Prospect Every day

I'm not much of a reader, but since I began my career in real estate I have been introduced to many wonderful books on business and self-improvement. One of these books that I highly recommend is, "The Compound Effect", written by Darren Hardy. One of the stories in the book, "The Story About the Penny", absolutely blew my mind.
(If you would like to see my suggestion of good real estate and motivational books, here is a link:
williejmayenterprises.com/recommended-reads)

Let me ask you a question: If you could have $3 million right now, this second, in cold hard cash, or $0.01 that doubles every day for 31 days, which would you choose? Think about that for a second.

You might have heard this…... "For every day you prospect, it will pay you back sometime in the future. And for every day you do not prospect you will lose that opportunity forever". My broker continuously reminds me to "Build on my Successes". Once you have that real estate momentum going it becomes easier to get more business. That's why prospecting every day is so important. You build on each day's successes. You become used to your schedule. You have a need to prospect, to follow up, to make relationships happen. You'll see your efforts mature into closed transactions. Your daily prospecting is like The Compound Effect.

Which one did you choose? The $3 Million or the $0.01 that doubles every day for 31 days? With the power of The

Compound Effect, did you know that after 31 days that single penny will transform into $10,737,418? When I first read that I couldn't believe it! I had to look it up, but incredibly the math works out.

- Day 1: $0.01
- Day 5: $1.00
- Day 10: $5.12
- Day 15: $163.84
- Day 18: $1,310.72

After day 18 you'll start to see how The Compound Effect begins really working its' magic.

- Day 20: $5,242.88
- Day 25: $167,772.16
- Day 28: $1,342177.28 Can you believe it? On day #28 it hit over a Million!
- Day 30: $5,368,709.12 The 30th day, it's now over 5 Million Dollars!
- Day 31: The last day, with The Compound Effect is fully in force. The penny has reached a whopping $10,737,418.23!

Wow, that's amazing!

It's an incredible story, but the numbers do not lie. I cannot stress this enough, that if you get into a habit where you are prospecting daily, you can use The Compound Effect to your advantage. The more people you contact, the more people you adopt into your database, and the more people that get to know you, like you, and trust you, turns into people who will call on you when it's time to sell, or refer you to a friend. This will be the foundation of your business.

The wonderful thing about prospecting is that it works for all types of clients. For sale by owners, expired listings, centers of influence, database, and follow-ups. Have you ever wondered why top-producing agents still have business when the market shifts? It's because of their dedication to prospecting. You can almost say, that if you prospect daily, you will have a recession proof business.

Agent Mindset

Agent mindset. Let's think about that for a moment. How do you feel about for sale by owner sellers? When you think of a FSBO do you get excited? Anxious? That you just can't wait to get in front of them to show them your system for putting more money in their pocket? Your system for getting their home sold faster than they thought possible, so they can move on with their dreams? Or are you the complete opposite? Scared, frightened, or frustrated? Are you unclear on the proper way to help them sell their home? If they're able to sell their home without a real estate agent, obviously they'll make more money, right? It must be true. It makes sense on paper, and that's what you tell yourself. So whenever you see a for sale by owner seller, do you turn tail and run?

Or maybe all the old veteran real estate agents in your office brainwashed you into thinking for sale by owner sellers are hard to work with. That they don't have any money, and they don't appreciate the value of a real estate agent. Or that you just cannot sustain a profitable business working with FSBO sellers. They've told you to just stay away from them and work your center influence and wait for the phone to ring. Let me ask you something... how that's working out for you?

This chapter on F.E.A.R. is to help you change your mind set about for sale by owner sellers. In the beginning of this chapter, I shared a few acronyms of F.E.A.R. One of those acronyms was: False Evidence Appears Real.

This acronym perfectly describes most agents' emotions when it comes to dealing with for sale by owner sellers.

So here it is in a nutshell: My Top 5 Suggestions to Overcoming Fear in Working with FSBOs.

#1 Affirmations: Have you ever heard the expression, "Whether you think you can, or you think you can't... you're right". Success is all about believing in yourself and knowing that no matter how many times you fall down, you must get back up and dust yourself off. Tell yourself you're going to make it. One of the best things that helped me to believe in myself was doing daily affirmations. Say some in the morning over coffee, in the middle of the day, or just before you go to sleep at night, and eventually they'll sink in and become a part of who you are.

I suggest you go on the internet and look up some affirmations that will help you believe in yourself and give you the power to know that no matter what happens in your life or who you encounter, you're the man or woman in charge of your own life. Here is a link to a YouTube video of an affirmation that I find inspiring. I strongly advise you use a headset when listening to this affirmation.
 Multi-Million Top Producing Real Estate Professional - MOTIVATIONAL POWERFUL AFFIRMATIONS

#2 Study the Market: Be on top of your game and study your market. Know what the average sale price is in your area. Know what types of homes are selling where you work. Colonial? Traditional? Spanish style? Be familiar with the home builders in your area, past and present. Learn the different styles of homes and floor plans each area builder produces and which are the most popular.

I know of one agent who took it a bit further, and for every property he sold, if the original owner was in possession of the floor plans which the builder gave them, he would purchase those plans from the owner. Wow. Talk about going the extra mile. Imagine showing up at a FSBO property and having the floor plan to their style of home. That will definitely set you apart.

Know your area better than any other real estate agent. The average sales price, the absorption rate, times and places of the neighborhood book club or HOA meetings. Go one step further and double down on the information. For example: know which days the trash company comes to pick up the trash and recyclables. What are the names of different schools in the area, and how do they compare to other schools in the state? (You can find this information at greatschools.org.) Being well-informed and up-to-date on available information will allow your clients to have more faith and trust in your ability to do your job well.

Knowing the area that you work in will give you confidence when working with FSBO sellers or any client for that matter and will allow you to be prepared for any off-the-wall questions that may pop up.

#3 Be Consistent: That's right, be consistent. Being a successful real estate agent means putting in the work. Nights, weekends, whenever you have a spare moment, you need to put in the hours now, so you can be on cruise control tomorrow. It's kind of like when you first started in real estate, or when you're recovering from a sales slump... you're like a rocket ship on the pad just about to launch, but you need to make sure you're fueled up and ready when that timer counts down to zero. Make sure all systems are go before you take off!

Once you blast off it means putting in the work Monday mornings through Sunday nights; open houses on weekends; knocking on doors and making those cold calls. You're laying down the foundation of your success, and it is NOT going to happen overnight. Develop a schedule and reach out to potential clients consistently. Put it on your daily agenda, say from 8 to 11:30, that you're on the phone making those calls, and again in the afternoon if you have spare time. Always remember that slow and steady wins the race.

#4 Work on your Scripts and Dialogues: I know in the beginning I was scared to death talking to for sale by owner sellers, because I did not know what to say. That's why you need to develop a dialogue and memorize it. Most of the time, people who are trying to sell their own home have one main reason for it: To save money. It's basically their one main objection to hiring an agent. Once you understand that there's really very few reasons for FSBO objections, it will be easier to create a dialogue addressing these few issues, and you'll become more confident in your ability to talk to these potential clients and put their minds at ease. This will also make it easier for you to pick up that phone and dial that number and make that appointment.

Just about everyone these days has a Facebook account, so ask your friends for help; or you may have someone in your office that you can partner with to role-play and go over your scripts. The more you practice your dialogues with other people, the better you'll become at talking to for sale by owner sellers, or any potential client for that matter. It will also boost your self-esteem, and make your work more exciting, rewarding, and even fun!

#5 Get started....NOW! That's right get started RIGHT NOW! Well, right after you finish this book or audible book at least. Then drop everything and get on those phones!

Conquer your fears and those FSBO sellers. All joking aside, the main advantage of starting right now is that you're putting your real estate business FIRST and getting a jump on the competition.

You: "But William, I don't know exactly what to say. I'm scared on the phone. What if they say 'yes, I'm ready to sell, come over,' and I don't know what to do?"

Don't worry! I've been through this, and every other agent in the world has been through this, and we've all survived. You're not alone. Picking up that phone the first time may be one of the hardest things you ever have to do, but sooner or later you're going to have to do it if you want to be successful in this business. You bought this book, so it's obvious you're looking for help and information that will help you to succeed. But the secret to success that you're looking for is right inside yourself. You alone have the power to succeed in your own life and your own career. I am merely providing you the information and the tools and resources to help make that climb a little easier, but I can't do the work for you. I can put a million dollars in front of you, but unless you take it and spend it or invest it or burn it, it's not going to do you or anyone any good.

Unfortunately, failing is sometimes a part of real estate. It's an uphill climb, but each step takes you closer to your goal. You're going to make a lot of calls. And occasionally you're going to find FSBO sellers that aren't ready or willing to work with you. Sometimes they may not even like you or care to give you a chance, and some will just hang up on you.

Unfortunately, that's just part of the game. Just keep in mind that you're reaching out to people who DO actually want to sell their home, so if you continue to follow-up with them and show them just how invaluable of an agent you are, then over time you WILL win them over. And eventually you will see that working with for sale by owner sellers is not as hard and scary as other agents may have made it seem. Maybe it was just difficult for them because they didn't invest the time and effort into those potential clients that you're willing to invest.

To make a long story short, it all basically comes down to consistency, hard work, and persistence. Just make sure that you make your calls every day, practice your scripts and dialogues, and research your sales area. Over time your skills will get better, your dialogue will become second nature, and before you know it all the fears that you once had about contacting for sale by owner sellers will be but a distant memory.

Chapter 3: Working with FSBO's Successfully

When you start working in real estate, or rather, when you actually make up your mind that you want to be SUCCESSFUL in real estate, you should pick a few prospecting niches to focus your time and effort on. In this way, when you're lead generating, you're maximizing your time to generate the best results.

FSBO leads are my favorite evergreen leads. Unlike other real estate markets that come and go at the drop of a hat, there is always a steady supply of For Sale By Owner Sellers! There may be one today, and five tomorrow. But one thing's for sure: no matter what your real estate market, FSBO leads will always be a consistent source of business.

Now with that said, you have to know how to work FSBO sellers, because they're not your typical lead. I like to think of for sale by owner sellers as a fine wine. All good or exceptional wines must be aged appropriately for the maximum best taste when you drink it. In that same way you must develop a relationship with these potential clients. Get to know them, give thoughts and ideas time to age, and let them breathe.

If the seller has a $300,000 home and you're being paid a 6% commission, that equals out to $18,000. That's a lot of money coming out of the seller's pocket. No matter what you say to the seller, it will fall on deaf ears unless they actually try the selling process on their own. Eventually they're going to realize that it's not as easy as it seems. Always remember "Telling is not Selling". There is no better teacher than experience.

Never forget that working with For Sale By Owner sellers is a long game. You may have to follow up anywhere from 8 to 20 times in order to convert to a sale, and this may vary in different real estate markets.

Remember this when you're trying to work with a FSBO

- Give the seller time to get to know you.
- Give the seller time to get to like you.
- The seller needs to realize they can trust you.

No FSBO will work with you if they don't know you, like you, and/or trust you. The simplest, most effective way to work with For Sale By Owner Sellers is just to stay in contact with them once a week from the initial contact. This is not rocket science; it's not brain surgery. It's so simplistic that I'm unsure why it's extremely hard for 90% of the agents out there to get it. They believe there has to be something more to it, but there isn't.

I'm sure you've heard the saying…. "The money is in the follow up." The main ingredient in working with For Sale By Owner Sellers is Your Follow-Up!

FSBO Mindset

An additional key to working with for sale by owner sellers is that you have to understand their mindset, and their typical mindset is: "I want to sell my property on my own, so I can save as much money as possible". I stated this in my introduction into this book, and that we are living in a Do-It-Yourself day and age, where people feel like they can and should handle all aspects of their lives themselves.

I'm not sure about you, but if there's a way for me to save tens of thousands of dollars by doing something myself, then I'm all for it. But what FSBO sellers don't realize is that saving that money by not paying a commission may look good on paper, but they're actually losing more than they think.

And that's our job, isn't it? To be an asset to our potential clients and help them with the things they do NOT realize.

There are basically THREE types of FSBO sellers:

#1 The Newbie:
They believe that selling real estate is easy, no problem, and anyone can do it! For Sale sign in the yard? Check! Ad in the local paper? Check! Craigslist ad? Check! Schedule an open house this weekend? Check! They're so excited, yet so naive, that they think once they hold that open house, potential buyers will just show up with bags and bags of cash.

#2 The Seasoned Seller:
These sellers have been in the game for a while. They can see a real estate agent coming from a mile away. They are an "expert" when talking to agents, and they have their own scripts and dialogues memorized. "Can you bring me a buyer? What's your commission? Will you take 2%? Another agent said they would". And the list of objections goes on and on.

(The answer to that 2% objection is, of course, "No, Sir. Let me ask you, how many weeks out of the year do you work for your boss for free? If we decide to work together, I'm sure we can negotiate a commission that is fair to both of us and still allows the house to sell. I would love to take a look at your home. Would today at 5:00 work, or would 6:30 be better?")

#3 The Burnt-Out Seller:

The fast cash and easy sale of his home that he imagined in the beginning has become a distant memory. This seller no longer answers his phone calls but screens them. He no longer listens to voicemails, but deletes them a whole batch at a time, because he or she has come to the realization that the only people calling about their property are more real estate agents wanting to take the listing. This for sale by owner seller is on the brink of throwing in the towel.

The burnt-out seller is just frustrated, and expectedly so. With a little practice rehearsing your scripts and some on-the-job training calling FSBO sellers, you'll have a higher probability of converting them in stage 2 and 3 of this example. The key is consistent follow-up. If you've been contacting them since they listed their home, or close to it, and you've been contacting them once or twice a week since then, you've been building a rapport with them, and are better able to answer their questions. Maybe you even had the opportunity to stop by during their open house, or you were able to set an appointment to preview the property. All of this hard work and dedication adds up to a potential listing.

I want to be clear here, I am not guaranteeing you any type of results. Your results will vary from state to state, market to market, seller to seller. Nothing in this life is guaranteed, as we all know. But you can't succeed if you don't work the system. All you need to do is pick up the phone every day and make your calls, and don't ever give up. And if you follow these examples of hard work, dedication, and consistency, then there's NO reason why you wouldn't or can't succeed.

Chapter 4: Frequently Asked Questions

Where do I get the numbers?
There are several different services to get FSBO numbers or numbers in general in the real estate business. There are not as many landlines as there were back in the day, but there ARE websites.

I've tried several different FSBO services. In my opinion you should try various services and find out which ones work best for you and your market.

FSBO services: (In no particular order)

1. Zillow.com
2. Trulia.com
3. Red X
4. Land Voice
5. Vulcan7
6. Rebo Gateway
7. Mojo Sells-Lead store (I personally use and endorse)
8. Espressoagnt.com
9. Forsalebyowner.com
10. Fizber.com
11. 4salebyowner.com
12. Fsbo.com
13. Fsbo-home.com
14. Hotpads.com
15. byownerdaily.com

And the list goes on and on. When you're prospecting FSBO sellers, understand that they're a different beast. You may have to cold call hundreds, even thousands of numbers to get in touch with someone who may be thinking about selling their home sometime in the near future.

But on the other hand, when you do find them, they're hot, they're ready, and they want to sell NOW! How many cold calls do you have to make before you run into a client who's looking to sell? How many doors do you have to knock? How many people in your database do you have to call? How many expired listings do you have to check on or show up to, to finally get that listing? As many as it takes. When you finally find that seller, they're looking to sell RIGHT NOW. The only catch is they wanted to do it on their own. No problem! The hard part is already done: the searching, finding, and identifying a homeowner who's looking to sell. Now all you have to do is convince them that you should help them!

When it comes to selling real estate, the slogan I use in my advertising is "GET SOLD NOW". Out of all the leads out there other than the COME LIST ME LEADS, FSBOs are probably one of the best sources of ripe, low-hanging fruit listing businesses out there. Are you ready to harvest your success?

What is the best CRM to use?
So how do you decide which is the best Customer Relationship Management System (CRM) to use? Fellow real estate agents have been asking that question since the beginning of time. There are so many different kinds of CRM's out there that you're bound to find one that fits your needs. Some are more advanced than others, and some are super simplistic.

If you're a new agent, and you've found a simple, easy-to-use system to retrieve your data, then use it. Stick with it, and when you get to a certain level where you've mastered that system and want something more challenging or more powerful, that's when it's time to start experimenting with other, more advanced contact management systems.

If you're an agent that's been in the game for a while and you're tired of your current CRM, then experiment with other systems that are available. Usually they'll offer a free trial or some sort of promotion to get your precious business. Change it up and keep it fresh!

Need a few examples? How about Top Producer, Red X, Mojo Dialer, Infusionsoft, Salesforce, BoomTown, and the list goes on and on. You get the picture.

Well William, you may ask, what CRM do you use? I actually use two CRM's. Yes, I'm crazy like that. The truth is, for right now it's best for me to use two systems in my business, but eventually that may change. Like I mentioned earlier, you have to treat your business like a living, growing business. When it grows, you must grow with it.

I use the Mojo Dialer and Contactually. I have to give Mojo Dialer credit. In the last few years they have developed into a very powerful CRM with a 3-line dialer. I'm not going to go into detail. I primarily use Mojo for the dialing system to circle prospect: Cold calling, Expired, For Sale By Owners & My People Farm.

Contactually is the second CRM that I use. I enjoy their simple interface and their ease-of-use. I primarily use Contactually for working my Spear of Influence (SOI), and my database. Unfortunately, Contactually doesn't have a dialing system, but I don't hold that against them.

Just take your time and do your own due diligence. See which program best fits you, your business and your personality.

What is the best auto dialer to use?

You have Turbodial for Infusionsoft, Vulkan 7, Redx Storm Dialer, and quite a few others. The whole purpose of using an auto dialer is to be more efficient in your prospecting. There are many types of auto dialers. Some have a single line, and some have a multi-line set up.

If you're a new agent or just starting out calling For Sale By Owner sellers, I would suggest you start with the old-fashioned method. Use your cell phone, office phone, or your home phone. These are high-quality leads you do not want to lose because of a bad connection or a delayed connection.

When you're new at calling FSBO sellers, it's best to get comfortable with calling them one at a time. Do not rush it, just take your time. If you work with them in this way, your comfort level and experience in dealing with these sellers will increase. Only then would I suggest moving to an auto dialer.

My auto dialer of choice is the Mojo sales dialer. I can cold call and/or circle prospect with their 3-line dialer. The system can call up to 300 numbers per hour. It's a tremendous time-saver over calling one at a time on your own phone. And as an added bonus, if I don't have that many numbers to call, I can adjust the dialing system to 2 lines or 1. And just recently they added a new service called "Click-to-Call". Click-to-call gives you all the time you need to review the information before you click that button, and then it auto dials the client. (Thanks, Mojo, for adding that great feature!)

Another bonus in the Mojo system is that you can set up groups. I have divided For Sale By Owner Sellers into two groups: New For Sale By Owners, and Old For Sale By Owners. These groups helped me stay organized and on point when I'm prospecting my potential FSBO clients.

Should I Leave a Message?

When calling for sale by owner sellers, it is always good to leave a voicemail. Just make sure your voicemail is to the point, short and sweet.

Example: "Hello, my name is William May, and I'm a real estate agent with Happy-Go-Lucky Real Estate. I see that your home is for sale by owner. Congratulations! I've seen your ad, and I have a few questions regarding your home. As I'm sure you know, most homes like yours sell quickly. Is your home still available? If so, would it be available for a viewing if I have any buyers that are interested in your particular home? You can contact me at 323-123-4567. Thank you for your time and have a great day!"

As you can see this message is short, polite, and to the point, and identified a few key subjects. First, I identify myself as a real estate agent. Second, I let them know that I'm aware that the home is for sale by the owner of the property, and also showing some enthusiasm by saying congratulations! This lowers their guard a little bit, so I don't just seem like another agent wanting to take their listing.

Thirdly, I'm letting the homeowner know the reasons for my call: that I have a few questions regarding the property. They become curious because they already know that I've seen their ad since I told them I did, so the most common questions should already be answered. (That is if the ad was written correctly.) So, this peaks their curiosity and gives them a reason to speak with me.

In my experience, when I first started cold calling without a dialer, leaving messages took a lot of my time. But I received 2 great listings from cold calling, and one I was able to double end. So, leave messages like you're playing the lottery, because you can't win unless you play!

Should I Tell the FSBO Seller That I Have a Buyer When I Really Don't?

Absolutely not! You do remember your code of ethics, correct? If you want to be successful in this business, you always need to be up front and honest. Yes, sometimes that may hurt your pocketbook. As for myself, I'm not going to sell my soul to the devil for a commission check. People are selling the most expensive and valuable asset in their lives. They need to work with an agent who is honest and trustworthy and is always looking out for their best interest. Always keep your integrity intact. Your reputation depends on it.

Chapter 5: Do You Have The Drive And Determination to Succeed?

Do you think you have what it takes to succeed in this crazy, mixed-up world of real estate? As of 2018 the real estate industry is ranked 12th in agent turnovers. Mainly because most real estate agents entering into the business are not fully prepared for the reality of the real estate market. They are so used to working nine-to-five jobs, and having a boss looking over their shoulder to make sure they stay on track and do what they need to do. But once they enter into real estate there is no accountability. You have to look over your own shoulder and keep yourself on track.

In most brokerages they give you a cubicle, The Haines directory, and tell you…. "Good luck, make those calls!" Then they throw you in the deep end, and it's sink or swim. If you learn to swim, great! You make yourself, your family, and their broker money, and all is good in the world. But if you don't, you drown, and eventually become a distant memory. The good news is, it doesn't have to be that way! Real estate can be an easy, fun, and wonderful business to grow in. But it takes commitment, learning, and... oh yes, a whole lot of hard work. Remember, nothing worth having comes easy, and nothing that comes easy is worth having. Here are a few tips to help your drive and determination kick in for success.

Consistency

You can do open houses, door-knocking, and phone prospecting. The best thing you can do is to get face-to-face, belly-to-belly, with as many potential customers as you can. And once you have a steady flow of income, then you can take the weekends off to spend more time with your family. And believe me…. that's priceless!

It's a Numbers Game!

Did you know that the numbers are in your favor? Did you know that homeowners are 70% more likely to use the first agent that they come in contact with? Sounds like good news to me!

I don't understand a lot of these coaches and trainers who throw out these ridiculous numbers like, "For every 10 FSBO you call, you'll get one listing" or something ridiculous like that. I believe in real world numbers, and it's not that pretty, or that easy. Being successful, like I say, is hard work.

These numbers are just an example of the worst-case scenario. As you know, your results may vary, but once you start the process and get more familiar with your prospecting style and contact ratio, the numbers will develop a pattern that you can use to build your successful business.

For example, let's say you have to dial 100 numbers to get 2 contacts.
And let's say you need 100 contacts to generate 2 good leads.
And let's say you need 50 good leads to generate 1 appointment.
And let's say you need to make three appointments to take just one listing.

See how the number game works? If you're not fortunate enough to be like some of these uber successful real estate agents who seem to have an armored truck full of cash to pay for marketing, mailers, and retargeting ads to retrieve their business, then you're just going to have to prospect. To hustle like any other hungry real estate agent that wants to succeed.

The hardcore truth is, you need to first focus on the basics: Coming into the office early every morning, practicing your scripts, role playing with other agents, and you stay on that phone all day long if you have to. Eventually you'll become a master at telephone prospecting. And then you move on to door knocking, open houses, or whatever form of prospecting you feel comfortable with. Master it, and be consistent with it, and eventually you WILL be a success.

Chapter 6: Tools You Will Need

Your Calendar

Either a physical calendar, or a digital calendar, or both. The calendar is one of the main tools for being successful in real estate. Become accustomed to scheduling everything in your calendar. Spending time with the family, doctor and dentist appointments, your family vacations. Anything and everything must go into the calendar, so that you can stay on track with your business and know when you can be available to potential clients.

Make sure most importantly that you schedule your prospecting as a recurring appointment. And do NOT schedule your listing appointments during prospecting hours. The only exception to the rule is if you're new or you're in a sales slump. Then, of course, drop everything and get that listing!

Workstation

You'll need a quiet and distraction-free work environment. This could be anywhere in your home or work office. Just anywhere you can be productive without distractions.

Computer or Laptop

In this tech-savvy world, I don't see how it's even possible to have a real estate business without a computer. The computer or laptop doesn't have to be state-of-the-art or have all the bells and whistles known to man. Just as long as you have a digital device that will help you prospect. I mainly work off of my home PC. At the office I use my laptop simply because it's very mobile and convenient if I have to pick up and go to a conference room or to a meeting in another agent's office.

I also use an iPad on the go. This is very convenient for me for several reasons. I could use it at a meeting, or at a business lunch, or for general prospecting on-the-go, which allows me to log into my Mojo dialing system or into my CRM. I also take it with me on listing presentations, just in case I need to show clients a detail about comparable sales in the area.

Telephone

It is a must to have a good reliable smartphone. It doesn't matter if it's Apple, Samsung, Motorola or a BlackBerry. As long as you have a phone that is dependable, with good service and a good data plan, so you can conduct your business in a professional manner.

Your Car

I want you to understand this, you don't need a $100,000 BMW to be successful in real estate. Make do with what you have, and upgrade if necessary, once the means become available. However, it is imperative that you have dependable transportation.

Chapter 7: FSBO Objections

There is definitely a system to the madness. No matter what script you decide to use, your end goal is the same: to generate appointments, to determine if a lead is worth following up, or if the lead is trash. The reflex answer to objections is usually no, so in the first part of the conversation most of the time you can just shelve that objection. If it is serious enough the client will bring it back up later in the conversation, and that's where you have to make a decision on the best way to handle that objection.

Always repeat, affirm, and then ask another question. Mirror and match the client. Let the potential client speak 80% of the time, and you only 20% of the time, mostly with questions. Statistics have shown that the more someone talks and asks questions, the more rapport you build. Focus on their needs that wants but keep the endgame in mind. Knowing your scripts and dialogues is not enough. You must practice them. The more prospecting that you do, the better you will be with your communication.

Top 10 Objections

#1 I Only Work with Buyer's Agents.

#2 I Can Sell the House on My Own, I've Done it Before.

#3 I Cannot Afford to Pay Your Commission.

#4 Will You Cut Your Commission?

#5 I Will Use a Discount Broker and List It on the MLS.

#6 We Already Have an Agent We Will Use if We Can't Sell on Our Own.

#7 We Will Use Our Family Member Who is an Agent.

8 Do You Have a Buyer?

#9 Bring Me a Buyer and I Will Pay 3%.

#10 What Are YOU Going to do Differently to Sell My Home?

#11 Bonus Objection: What's Your Commission?

Chapter 8: Top 10 FSBO Objections

1. I Only Work with Buyer's Agents.

A) OK great, now let me make sure I have this correct... You're only willing to work with buyer's agents, correct? (Yes.) Is that agent working for you or the buyer? (The buyer.) So, if you take a second to think about it, the buyer's agent is not looking out for your best interests, only the buyers' best interests, correct? (Yes.) So how about this: Let's make an appointment for me come over and see your home. This way we can discuss some options on selling your home for the most money, and make sure that we have YOUR best interests at heart. Does this make sense? (Yes.) Fabulous! I'll be in your area around 3 today or would 4 be better for your schedule?

B) Wow, only with buyer's agents? May I ask, how you feel that will help your bottom line?

(Notice how I acknowledged what they said, then immediately I intentionally asked another question. This is what you call "Shelving That Objection". It's like a reflex NO. Another point to remember is that he/she that asks questions maintains control of the conversation.)

C) OK, great. You only work with buyers' agents. I can understand that, but let me ask you a quick question... I have plenty of experience helping people such as yourself to sell their homes and have the buyers fight over the privilege of purchasing them. If I can show you a proven system where your home will not sit on the market, but will sell quickly for top market value, would you at least want to hear about it?

(If they say yes, set an appointment. If they say no, which in most cases they will, but not all the time, send them a thank-you card and follow up once a week until they say... stop contacting me! Or until they list with another agent. Remember that working with FSBO sellers is a matter of rapport and familiarity. They have to understand and believe your continuous communication is in their best interest. Once they realize that it is, along with getting to know you, they will list with you. Why? Because you have earned their trust.)

2. I Can Sell the House on My Own, I've Done it Before.

A) Hey that's great! I sell homes all day, every day as well. Like my father used to say, "If you love your what you do, you'll never have to work a day in your life." (Shelf the objection and move on) So when this home sells, where are you moving to?

B) Congratulations! I don't have to tell you that selling a property is not as easy as it looks. I/We, this year alone, sold over 25 homes. Our success comes partly from our networking with Top Buyers Agents, my/our marketing plan, and my skills as a negotiator. Let me ask you, if I can show you a proven plan to sell your home for top dollar, do all the work for you, and make this the smoothest transaction possible, would you want to hear more about it?

(If your production is not that high, just use your company stats as your market stats)

C) Hey that's wonderful. What all are you doing to market your home? (Shelved objection and keep asking questions.)

3. I Cannot Afford Your Commission.

A) I understand exactly where you're coming from. Most FSBO sellers believe that at first, so they try to sell on their own, believing they can make more money that way. Unfortunately, they eventually come to the realization that it is not as easy as it looks, and in the meantime, they have wasted their valuable time, money, and effort.
I'm just curious, if you're able to put some real money in your pocket, are you serious about selling your home?   (Yes.)
Okay. I'm not in the habit of wasting anyone's time, yours or mine, so let me suggest this: I'll do my homework on your property and the market. I'll give you a call back and let you know all the information I recovered, and then we'll see if we can go the next step. And if not, no harm, no foul. I'll keep in touch with you and be a resource for you and your family until the time is right. What do you say?

(When you get this objection sometimes it can be tricky because they may not have enough equity to sell, and if that's the case it is no longer an objection but is now a condition. A condition is something you cannot overcome at that specific time. But as is in this example, if they're low on equity that can change if/when the property value rises.)

B) I completely agree with you that selling your house using an agent such as myself is definitely a sizeable investment. But on the other hand, if I can show you with my proven system that I can sell your home for top dollar, and have it more than cover the cost of my commission, would you want to hear more about it?

C) I'm not one to argue, you have a valid point. Quick question: If there was a way, I could show you that I can sell your home for top market value and net you enough money to move forward with your family's plans, would you like to hear more about it? (Yes.) Great! I could pop by today at 5:00, or does 6:30 work better for your schedule?

(Always understand it doesn't matter what they tell you... I cannot afford to pay your commission, I don't want to pay any commission at all, your rates are too high, etc. Most of the time when they say these types of things, they are the same statements that they used to get rid of the last agent, so you have to ask questions to find out exactly where they stand. Set yourself apart from past agents. Ask questions and get to know their particular situation. It may be the case that they simply cannot pay your commission. That would be a condition, not an objection. Sometimes you just have to let a lead go and move on to the next. It's the nature of the business.)

4. Will You Cut Your Commission?

A) Commissions in the state of California are completely negotiable. Are you familiar with how commissions work in relation to selling your home? (No.) Okay, let's kill two birds with one stone. Let me pop by, take a look at your house, and I can answer any questions you may have regarding commission or anything related to selling your house in this real estate market.

(When it comes to answering questions about commission, it

can be a very touchy subject. You're not going to win a listing by simply answering their question over the phone. Always remember to acknowledge their question, immediately ask another question, or shelve the objection. Keep the conversation moving towards your ultimate goal, which is setting an appointment.)

B) That's a great question. I'm willing to work for whatever price we can agree to. Let me ask you, when you sell this home, where is your family moving to next?
(Keep the conversation moving by answering and immediately asking another question.)

C) Let me ask you a question: How many weeks out of the year do you work for your boss for free?
(Wait for their response. And remember, the first person that speaks, loses.)
I'm a very aggressive agent when it comes to working with my clients. Part of my job as your agent is being a good negotiator. If I can not negotiate my commission with you, how would I be able to negotiate the best price for your home with a potential buyer?

Offer to set up a time when you can take a look at their home. Include things like, "Once I see what type of property I'm working with, we can discuss a commission that works best for you, for me, and still allows the home to sell for top dollar. Fair enough?"

D) I'm willing to work for whatever amount we can agree to, and that will depend on a few things, such as.... current market conditions, condition of the property, the asking price for the property, and how long you give me to sell it. I'm sure when we meet, you will be very impressed with how I do business.

I like to meet with people in the afternoons or evenings. Just be sure to ask what day and time of day would work best for them.

(In my opinion the commission objection is the most difficult objection for agents to handle. If you make time in your schedule to practice role playing and rehearse with other agents, this or any other objection should no longer be an issue for you.)

5. I Will Use a Discount Broker and List it on the MLS.

A) So, you want to use a discount broker and put it on the MLS, is that correct? (Yes.) I'm just curious, in your opinion how does that strategy help you and your family get your property sold? (Basically, they'll tell you it's by saving the commission or something of that nature.)

Okay, I see, and I can understand your point. It looks good on paper. But what if I could show you a way that I could save you time, money and effort, and most importantly SELL your house quickly, all the while putting the MOST money in your pocket? If that was possible, you would definitely be open to hearing more about that, wouldn't you? (How could they not say yes?)

B) Am I hearing you correctly, discount broker? (Yes.) May I ask, what will he or she do differently than myself to get your home sold? (Basically, they won't know how to answer this question. The only thing they may say is: the commission is cheaper / there is a cheap flat fee / the agency will list it on the MLS, or something to that effect.)

To which you reply, "I see. Have they provided you with a written guarantee that they will not charge you a dime unless your home sells?" (No.) Then let's do this, I don't mind... I can pop over today and show you my proven system that has helped many of my clients get their home sold quickly for top dollar, and with this system you'll see that I don't charge you anything until your home is sold.

Would you be available today at 5 or would 6:30 be better for your schedule? (This forces them to choose a time for that appointment.)
Be sure to get their email address so you can send them more information about yourself and your sales system and share your contact information with them as well.

C) In my experience, most of my clients use a discount broker because they're looking to save the most money. Is that the case for you? (Yes.)
That makes sense to me. Let me just send you my marketing plan so that way you can compare my proven system to their marketing plan. In this way, you can make an educated decision on which company is going to net you the most amount of money.

You are looking to put the most money in your pocket when you sell your home, aren't you? (Yes I am, but they have not provided me with any kind of marketing plan.) Wow, they haven't? I know most companies just charge a flat fee, post your property on MLS, and basically tell you to sit back for a couple months until your home sells for a discounted price.

This is called Post and Pray. Are you looking to sell your property for a discounted price? (Hell no!) Then how about I send you my proven marketing plan, so that you can see exactly how I get my clients' homes sold for top dollar? What's your email address? (Hot-home-seller@gmail.com) Okay great. I'm available this evening between at 5:00 and 7:00. What time would be best for you?

Valuable Tip: This extra step works wonders: After you set the appointment and email them your pre-listing package or your marketing plan, have a messenger or courier service deliver your package. Make sure it arrives before the scheduled appointment. Ideally you want to have it delivered within 2 hours of speaking to them.

When you're dealing with listings out here in Southern California where prices are $400,000 and up, you get up out of your chair and deliver the package yourself. I have even paid an Uber driver many times to deliver my pre-list package. These special touches will put you head and shoulders above your competition.

I am currently working on the course that teaches you how to make your own Pre-List Package & Marketing Plan. If you're interested, please email me at: Williejaymay@gmail.com

6. We Already Have an Agent We Will Use If We Can't Sell on Our Own.

A) Okay, I can understand that you're going to use someone that you already have in mind. (I am shelving that objection) How long will you be trying to sell your property on your own before you decide to use an agent? (Maybe 2 weeks.) Hey, that's great.

Are you willing to work with agents that can bring you a buyer? (Yes, we will pay 3%.) You will pay 3% to a buyer's agent, that makes sense. Our office has over a hundred and fifty agents. On average each of our agents are usually working with two or three buyers at a time. I would love to stop by your property to take a look at it. This way we can meet in person and I can see what type of home you have to offer to potential buyers.

I like to meet with people in the early afternoons or on weekends. I can pop by today at 5 or would Saturday at 2 work best for your schedule?

B) I completely understand. I've been in the real estate game for a while now, and almost everyone has at least one person in their family or circle of friends that is an agent or knows an agent.

Quick question... if I had a buyer who's willing to pay full price for your home, and is in the position to close within 30 to 45 days, would that be of some interest to you? (Sounds great, but do you actually have a buyer?)

Possibly, but I don't know because I haven't seen your house yet. I'll be in your neighborhood today between 4:30/5:00. How about I stop by and take a look at your home, so I can see exactly what you have to offer for today's buyers. I can also show you exactly how I get homes sold for top market value with my marketing plan, proven to attract buyers who are looking for properties just like yours. So, would 5:00 work for you? I'd love to show you how I can get your home sold in the next 30 to 45 days.

7. We Will Use Our Family Member Who Is an Agent.

I can almost anticipate what's going through your mind right now as you read that objection. 90% of real estate agents hear this objection and hang up the phone right away. That's understandable, because 80% of the time when you hear this objection, it's not really an objection. It's a condition. And the only way to find out if it's a condition or an objection is to make the call and have a conversation.

A) That's wonderful. It's always good to know someone in the business. I sell a lot of homes in the area, maybe I have worked with them in the past. What is their name? (Well, they do not really work in the area.)Ok, I have an idea. How about I pop by and take a look at your home, and show you how I sell my clients' homes for the most money, and if the numbers make sense to you maybe we can work out a referral for your family member? It's a win-win for everyone. I can pop by today at 5:00, or would 6:30 be better for your schedule?

B) That's great. It's always good to know someone in the business. I sell a lot of homes in the area, maybe I have worked with them in the past. What is their name? (James Calhoun, of ABC Realty right here in town. Have you heard of him?) No, I haven't heard of him, but I'm sure he's an excellent agent. Have you signed a listing contract yet? (No, not yet.)

In my experience it's always good to have two companies competing for your business, so you can determine which company best fits your needs and expectations. I highly respect that you're considering a family member, but keep in mind we are dealing with the most expensive asset most people own in their lifetime.   How about I just send you my marketing plan, and my proven system on how I show homes and get top dollar for my clients? This way you can compare my marketing plan with James', and you can make an educated decision on which agent is the best fit to sell your home. Make sense?

They can either say, "Yes, send me over your information", or they can say "No thanks, I'm just not interested". When they say no, simply reply with…. "It's been a pleasure speaking with you. If anything changes, please don't hesitate to call. Have a great day!" You might ask me, "William, with a conversation like this, after they've shut you down, would you still send them a thank you card?" The answer is always YES. No matter who you talk to, always take the time to send them a thank-you card. You never know what may happen in the future. I have had clients who sold their home with another agent, but because I sent them that thank you card, they sent me a referral. Real estate is funny that way, and that's why I love it.

C) That's great. It's always good to know someone in the business.   I sell a lot of homes in the area, maybe I have worked with them in the past. What is their name? (None of your business/you don't need to know. Do you have a buyer?) I don't know, maybe. I haven't seen the house yet. If I did have a buyer, are you willing to cooperate with buyers' agents? (Yes, but I'm only paying 2% and not a penny more!) Hey, that's great. Good luck and thank you for your time. Have a great day!

(Sometimes, inevitably, you'll run into people that have an attitude. Do not take this personally, it's just part of the job. They're not upset with you. Maybe they are upset because they're only receiving calls from agents and not buyers.

Maybe they're just having a bad day. Or maybe there has been a death in their family, and they're carrying the burden of trying to sell the house and handle the estate. Maybe they've lost their job and are being forced to sell a home that they love. All of these things can be extremely stressful, so when you're prospecting and calling FSBO sellers, keep an open mind, and always be compassionate to the people you speak to.)

8. Do You Have a Buyer?

A) Possibly. Our office has over 50 agent that work with an average of 3 buyers each. If we can generate a full price offer and get you sold and moved on with your life, that would definitely work for you and your family…...right?

B) Let me ask you, what type of buyer are you looking for? (No matter what they say, reply with the following.) Ok, we can both agree that the best buyer is someone who is ready and willing to pay your price and that can close escrow, correct? If I/we can generate that buyer and get you back on track with your original plans, are you ready to put me/us to work?

C) You know what, that's a good question. I can't answer right now, because I haven't even seen your house yet. Are you still interested in selling? (Continue with the script and set that appointment when appropriate.)

9. Bring Me a Buyer and I Will Pay 3%.

A) Okay, great! If I bring you a buyer, you're willing to pay a 3% commission, is this correct? (Yes.) Then it seems to me that we're on the same page. When would be a good time for me to come by and take a look at your home, so that I may show you exactly how I get my clients' homes sold for top dollar? I'll be in the neighborhood later on today. When would be the best time to pop by? This afternoon at 4:00, or would 5:30 be best for you?

B) A 3% commission, that's excellent. I'll make a note of that. By the way, you have a wonderful home. Would you happen to know how old the roof is? (Shelve the objection and continue on with your script, and when the time is right, close for the appointment.)

C) That's fantastic! Our office has over a hundred and fifty agents, and on average each agent is working with two or three buyers at a time, so I'm sure we can get your home sold. From what you've told me so far, it sounds like you have a wonderful home. When would be the best time for me to stop by and see it for myself? So that I can have an accurate idea of what you're offering the real estate market for today's buyers.

Work out an appointment time that works best for your seller and yourself and get down to business!

10. What Are You Going to do Differently to Sell My Home?

A) What am hearing you say is, how will I sell your home, when your last agent couldn't get the job done? Is this correct? (Yes.) Well, it is a detailed process. I would like to stop by this afternoon or evening to explain it you. What time would work best for you and your family?

B) Well, I am glad you asked. My office and I actually get homes SOLD. In the last 6 months or so, while your home was on the market, we SOLD over 125 homes! Would that be different? (Yes.) And do you know what the good news is, Mr/Mrs Seller? We can do the same for you and your family! Wouldn't that be great?

C) You would like to know how I am different from your last agent, and I can understand that. You've probably heard the saying, "telling is not selling". If you'll set a time for me to explain my plan for selling your home, I'll show you how I am different.

I would like to go over three things with you:

First, I would like to stop by to view your home and show you exactly why your home did not sell.

Second, I would like to show you a few things that will definitely draw in qualified buyers interested in paying top dollar for your home. Mr Seller, would you say that's pretty important for your bottom line? (Yes.)

The third thing I would like to show you is how we get results, while other agents' homes do not sell in this market place. Can we get together today at 5pm, or would 6:30 tomorrow be better for your schedule?

Bonus Objection: What Is Your Commission?

Tip: Never ever talk about commission before the appointment. If you do, you will lose whatever chance you have at setting that appointment and getting the listing. Trust me on this!

A) That's a great question. In the state of California, (or your state), the commission is negotiable, and that will be the first thing we will talk about when I see you.

B) Well, for now it's free!   What I mean by that is, I won't charge you a dime unless I/we get your home sold for the price and the terms you agreed to.

C) I am willing to work for whatever commission we can agree to that is fair for both of us, and that will depend on a few things, such as…

Current market conditions, condition of the property, how much you want for the property, and how long you will give me to sell it. I'm sure when we meet, you'll be amazed at how I/we do business.

D) Mr./Mrs. Seller, that's a great question. What I'm hearing you say is, you're really concerned about what you're going to net at the closing table, am I right?

E) Mr./Mrs. Seller, that will be the first thing we talk about when I see you. Our main goal is to use our proven system that will attract buyers who will pay top dollar for your home, and your main goal is to get the most money for your home, right?

F) I can definitely understand your concern. I have several commission structures. Let's find a time when we can get together and work out the numbers, so we can see what makes sense for you and your family. I'm sure, like most of my clients, you're not going to move forward unless the numbers make sense. (Close for the appointment.)

Chapter 9: Conclusion

Congratulations to you, for completing this book and taking the steps necessary to make your business a success! I'm proud of you! Not everyone can work for sale by owner sellers successfully. Reading this book, you now hopefully understand that it takes more than just learning scripts and objection handlers to be successful. You must have a thick skin, some brass balls, and the courage and strength to follow through.

I want you to understand more than anything, that you CAN succeed in real estate. You can do whatever you set your mind to. Do not let anyone take that away from you. I was fortunate enough to have a father that always encouraged me and told me I could overcome anything, no matter what the obstacle. He was right.

I would like to lay down a few more tips before you go, just to drive this home, and to make you understand that no matter what prospecting method you use, if you have made up your mind to succeed, YOU WILL SUCCEED! Remember these key ideas...

1) Believe in yourself and understand that you can do whatever you set your mind to do. Wake up early in the morning and say affirmations to yourself. Pray, meditate, or workout. Do what you need to do to obtain that peace in your mind, body, heart and spirit before you start your day, and your whole day will be better for it.

2) Prospect, prospect, prospect! No matter if you're calling FSBO, expired listings, cold calling, or door knocking. You HAVE to put in a minimum of 10 to 20 hours of actual prospecting every week to become successful in real estate on

a consistent basis. This is not busy work. This is actually talking to people on the phone or face to face and growing your business. If you're not doing this, you are not prospecting, and you are not using your time wisely.
3) Have your database get sick of you… in a good way, of course. Contact your database twice every quarter. Call them on their birthdays, anniversaries, holidays and all special events.
Once a month send them a postcard or use a service like realestatetools.com. Once a month, you could email them a neighborhood update on what homes have sold in the area, and at least once a quarter pop by their house just to say hi. Maybe even drop off a little gift if you would like.

Being successful in real estate is all about talking to people; interacting with them and helping them. Make those connections, and then grow those relationships. Put in the time and effort, and you can reap the rewards of your hard work later.

From the bottom of my heart I would like to thank each and every one of you who spent your hard-earned money, and most of all your valuable time, supporting me and reading this book or listening to the audible version. It shows your dedication to your craft and to your own success. To all of you, take care, and Godspeed to everything you touch. Thank You

I would like to say thank you for spending your hard-earned money purchasing this book, and most of all, for taking the time to learn the material inside it. We all need help from time to time, so I've included a few gifts for you.

Here are links to all of my courses. This is over 3 hours of content for less than $10 each. This is my way of saying "Thank You"!

Expired Listing Mastery 101
http://williejmayenterprises.com/thankyou101

New Real Estate Agent Business Plan
http://williejmayenterprises.com/bizplan

Open House Master Class for Real Estate Agents
http://williejmayenterprises.com/openhouse

Real Estate Agent Pre-List Package
http://williejmayenterprises.com/prelistpackage

William J. May

63960011R00035

Made in the USA
Middletown, DE
28 August 2019